Bountiful

for Peter + Jean,
with admiration
+ friendship
Michael
22 February 1992

Books by Michael Waters

Bountiful 1992
The Burden Lifters 1989
Anniversary of the Air 1985
Not Just Any Death 1979
Fish Light 1975

*Dissolve to Island: On the Poetry
 of John Logan* (Ed.) 1984

Bountiful

Michael Waters

Carnegie Mellon University Press
Pittsburgh 1992

Acknowledgments

America: "Moray Eels"
The American Poetry Review: "The Torches," "Miles Weeping"
Carolina Quarterly: "Creation," "Scotch and Sun," "The Lost
    Civilization"
Chelsea: "The Book of Tea," "At Homer's Tomb"
Crazyhorse: "Lace"
The Georgia Review: "The Difference Between a Rooster and a Whore"
The Gettysburg Review: "River Wife"
Ironwood: "Leeches"
The Journal: "Ticks"
Mississippi Review: "Portrait"
The Missouri Review: "Shadow Boxes," "The Fox"
The Ohio Review: "Betta splendens," "Village Dogs"
Poetry: "'Night in the Tropics' (1858-59?)," "Homo Sapiens,"
    "Bountiful," "Shhh," "The Inarticulate," "Hummingbirds,"
    "Paradys," "Scorpions"
Prairie Schooner: "Covert Street"
Quarterly West: "The Sadness of Barges"
River City: "Boy and Sycamore," "Snake Skin"
Shenandoah: "Singing for Elizabeth"
Southern Poetry Review: "Mosquito Nets"

"Miles Weeping" was reprinted in *Pushcart Prize XV: Best of the Small Presses,* edited by Bill Henderson (Pushcart Press, 1990).

"Covert Street" was reprinted in *Reading Rooms,* edited by Susan Allen Toth and John Coughlan (Doubleday, 1991).

I want to thank the Corporation of Yaddo and The Virginia Center for the Creative Arts for residencies, and the Maryland State Arts Council for Work-in-Progress Grants. Special thanks to Mary Gay Calcott and Sandra Poole for their friendship.

Publication of this book is supported by grants from the National Endowment for the Arts in Washington, D.C., a Federal agency, and from the Pennsylvania Council on the Arts.

Contents

for Kiernan

I have never known life without desire, and illusions sprang up afresh for me after every shipwreck of my hopes, for I was always dreaming of limbs, of gestures, of a voice more perfect still.
—Italo Svevo
Confessions of Zeno

"What are these outbursts of affection, Michael?" —Brett Ashley
—Ernest Hemingway
The Sun Also Rises

I

Creation

Vollard loved to tell his clients this story—

Degas, having arrived late for dinner,
paused with his host in the hushed, crowded parlor
—this host was a famous Parisian collector—
to view his painting recently hung there:
young ballerinas after rehearsal, sprawling backstage
or pivoted at the waist to untangle satin laces,
their hair cascading palest pinks and yellows,
exuding a weary, unself-conscious beauty.
Degas stared and stared till, without a word,
he lifted the picture in its gilt-edged frame
from its spot on the wall, the guests aghast,
then hefted it home under his arm
that he might retouch one dancer's limb.
He never returned the painting, never
passed near that gentleman's house again
while— here Vollard would clap his hands!—
all over Montmartre patrons of the arts
chained their Degas to their parlor walls.

Who hasn't been taught that a work of art
is never finished, but always "abandoned"?
Some tinker forever, souls fluttering in wrists,
allowing the light to surrender each stroke.

Imagine God's exhaustion once the earth
neared completion, before man was abandoned
to video arcades and two-story malls...

His infinite elation, the week's work gone well,
how He even transcended His own limitations—
then that inconsolable letdown, the probable certainty
that He could never again populate a planet
even if He took all of eternity, never again
bear to face such a vast, virginal
burnished white waste and,
beyond this, *how*
                    —the planet spinning now, luminous
as the archetypal pearl—
did He ever manage to float such a world?

"Night in the Tropics" (1858-59?)

*"Lack of listeners did not deter Louis Moreau
Gottschalk, living on the edge of a Guadeloupe
volcano in 1859, from giving piano recitals to
the universe."*   —Edmund Morris
                    "The Romance of the Piano"

Assuming *rain*, the exotic
species flare up like gas-flames
released from the earth, then settle on hibiscus
branches as the arpeggios shower down.
But the blossoms remain dry, their wings
dry, and only the spattering
notes keep them pinned to their trees, leaves
and insects blending in infinite
varieties.
            And the birds who pluck rare
butterflies from air, not finding them there,
assume *nightfall,* so return to their nests,
tongues stiff, though the sun slips
its staff of light through the canopies,
                              & so on
upward through the great chain of being, all
the bird-eating snakes, the snake-eating
birds, till the selection seems to halt,
Louis Moreau Gottschalk
slightly unnerved as he swabs the moisture
from the strings, shuts the lid of the Chickering,
then steps from the terrace into his room
to allow the universe to resume.

13

Homo Sapiens

Imagine a morning moon the color of cream
still steaming, a soul
newly-minted each exhalation of light,
omphalos quick with swirling aura.
Then the slow dissolve to absence.

Who can hold her?
Struck by the cold, the absolute
clarity of this nth morning of creation,
who might articulate this emotion
that somehow slipped past the masters, unnamed?

That creature whose skull was found
fragmented in lake-muck
more than one million years past her last
sigh— was she also struck by the icy
spill of moonlight so close to her cave
she might have stretched her fingers
toward its receding source?

Breasts milky in the afterglow,
she must have been beautiful, wild child,
stunned for a moment into consciousness.

The moon arcs now from that dawn to this,
passing over the bewildered
brilliance of van Gogh who brushed the moon
on thick to halt her travels,
over the unraveling intellect of Céline
who pinned the moon to a page
to prevent her passage even one night more.

But the moon forever fails over blight-scarred bark
while some early riser bears witness, fixed in the moment,
the day entered into
the log of creation by the soon-to-be forgotten
who tumble into passions
impossible to tame.

The wilderness remains with us.
The moon rises and beckons, leaving
a residue still too ancient to name.

II

Covert Street

The boy who lived in the library
slept among the stacks, behind long rows
of reference, awakening now and then to peek
from a gap in the book-bricked wall, one eye

gleaming across the marble floor or
his paste-scented breath feathering my neck
where I stood choosing three books from the profusion
ranging the stained and oaken shelves.

Three books were all the librarian would allow
a boy to carry home, only three
fingered from the festooned section for Young Readers,
yellow streamers framing their glossy spines.

I'd spend hours browsing those books, frowning
like the Hasidic fathers who suffered endless rounds
of chess in the park, rocking my bent body back
and forth till I finally made my choice.

I took my time because I loved the silence,
the scrubbed, glimmering aisles, the smell of lemon wax,
and the dust motes drifting through pillars of light
like snow through synagogue windows in the Carpathians.

A boy could breathe there, and never be bored.
He could learn to love his mother, those mournful
vowels, and his father, the harsh consonants,
then tender their names in a luminous language.

He could leave the library, as I did, as twilight
deepened, to begin the familiar walk home
with three books bracing his arm,
and count off each street, those eternal,

Brooklyn blocks he'd never forget
—Hancock, Halsey, Eldert—, then pause
when he came to his own, Covert Street
hushed in the breeze bowing the sycamores.

Boy and Sycamore

"I feel as though I had always worked that way;
face gazing at far things, hands alone."
—Rilke to Clara Westhoff, 1903

He is bored and so twists
the leaf-stems into braids, fingers
greening in the cloven dark, then stands
chipping bark for hours, it seems, each segment
the shape of a state, *Maryland, Ohio*,
leftover pieces of a jigsaw puzzle
that can't be forced to fit.

The boy doesn't choose to notice
the tremulous light, cumulus louring,
then the sun shouldering through bruised sky.
He leans with his cheek pressed against the grainy
striations of under-bark, the fragrant
folds, and whispers into the ear
the wet wood molds.

Soon his few friends join him.
As the day flames to depth, he brushes
the trunk with his uncombed hair and bellows
numbers into the numinous air beyond the branches'
quickening brocade. But the boy's kindled
mind is hushed: Leaf lisp. Bark banter.
The burgeoning language of the shade.

Singing for Elizabeth

How often have I tried to please you,
tracing your passage down Covert Street
where you floated, tenement goddess,
blown hair brushing the cypress branches,

floated with the joyful ease of the unborn,
raising my name to the Brooklyn rooftops,
calling to me among scorched tires and debris
that we might compare our inchoate desires?

My secret was the yearning, singular boyhood
I kept hidden, bruised marble, in my pocket.
Why should I have hurt you, imaginary twin,
made known that I slipped into this world alone?

That twelfth summer we wandered arm-in-arm,
counting couples in the abandoned schoolyard,
past the shattered mothers of the shoelace factory,
till you began to dissolve in the bell-struck breeze,

in the wishful dreaming, Elizabeth, gentle sister
who once touched your lips to my ear
to whisper: *Offer your solitude a name,*
then sing to her down the trash-lit alleys of air.

Shadow Boxes

in memoriam Joseph Cornell

*"The intense longing to get into the boxes
this overflowing, a richness & poetry felt
when working. . ."*

Six a.m. I'd be walking those sycamore-
   lined streets alone, red rubber
      ball in one hand, sawed-off

broomstick on my shoulder, waiting
   for a few friends to rise, morning
      to commence among parked cars

and manhole covers, the sun looming
   at last above tenement rooftops
      crisscrossed with clotheslines.

His slanted cellar-door would be propped
   open and I'd step down, eyes
      adjusting to the low

wattage, into the enormous clutter
   of his workshop, tables strewn with wire,
      paint-slick slats of wood, severed

dolls' heads, porcelain pipes, thimbles,
   tiny stoppered bottles cleansed
      of their lapsed medicines,

birds' nests, children's building-blocks,
   their letters sandpapered off,
      brass rings, ticket stubs, magazines—

the magazines!— tossed everywhere, 1940's
   illustrated ladies' weeklies, *National
   Geographics*, U.S. Army manuals,

storybooks and road atlases and astronomical
    charts, greeting cards bought
        bulk in boxes from thrift shops,

this world so dense with detail
    and populated with such familiar
        yet somehow exotic bric-a-brac

I'd forget I was below the thronged
    avenues of Flushing, 1964, my friends
        running bases on Utopia Parkway.

For hours I'd sit on a high stool
    with long scissors, turning pages,
        carefully clipping pictures—

parrots, Medici princes, even Lauren Bacall—
    while he pasted them in boxes
        of his own devising, concentrating

on each particular shade of blue, or
    the shape the paper made
        against a backdrop of winter stars,

but this morning he stopped, staring
    into the wreckage for something—
        he wasn't conscious of what—

until his glance chanced upon a ball
    balanced on a Coca-Cola bottle,
        and before I had the chance

to say *Wait, it's mine*, he'd placed it—
    just so— on two thin wires
        suspended over wineglasses, each

24

filled with a milky-blue cat's-eye marble,
and now we were done for the day,
at ease, sipping seltzer

before I returned to stifling streets
oddly empty, monochromatic,
lacking a certain delicacy

and playfulness, a world taken too
seriously in sunlight, intent
upon its own inviolability

as my eyes half-closed to glare
slashing off fenders and hoods
freshly washed and waxed

and buffed a metallic blue, but still
not the blue that blazed
below the earth, in darkness,

in a world where nothing would be lost,
where everything was given purpose,
if only it could remain patient.

The Difference Between a Rooster and a Whore

Those adolescent jokes blown from mouth
    to sour mouth, that sham
        resuscitation, the snickering
            gusts through schoolyards,
nudges and leers when the girls
    breezed by— are they still making
        their slow rounds, winding
            their way back to us, unchanged?
When I paused in the anonymous
    snow to piss obscenities
        in looping script, did I scrawl
            my name in the devil's book?
Last week on a crosstown bus
    a woman's umbrella snagged
        her skirt, the wire tugging
            toward mid-thigh. The driver,
glancing in the mirror, grinned
    at me, his bawdy buddy.
        Any cock'll do, the kids
            crowed, stoned on the pier
those sultry nights, gulping
    beer and shaking their cans
        to tease the hushed
            girls' hair with spray—
then hammered some fisherman's
    slimy haul: gasping eels,
        garbage fish, the frothing,
            vulgar mouth of the stingray.

Portrait

No man's face had ever been so red
    as my drunken uncle's fallen asleep
        under the sun lamp: a fire-engine

red, as if smeared with cheap
    lipstick, tube upon tube, "a face,"
        wrote Faulkner, "like a tragic marigold,"

though this face was redder, more exotic,
    an orchid ravaged on its frail
        stalk, the stigma radiating heat

—he'd let me touch— lightly!— his cheek—
    like the wooden matches struck
        with his thumbnail, their flared heads,

his one stylish Hollywood gesture
    in a brief life doomed to failure
        and cliché, his raw face finally

the impossible red of the amateur's
    palette, brilliant, useless, signifying
        passion beyond experience or technique.

So last week, loafing through some journal,
    abstract lyrics and fawning reviews,
        I found a memoir by the artist's model

Harriet Shapiro who'd posed for the realist
    Raphael Soyer not long before his death:
        "He had painted his soul on my face."

—Then I remembered that miserable uncle
    who slept without luck under the lamp's
        false coal when I still understood

nothing about the nature of art, the meta-
   physics of the soul, or how the human face
      can bear the stamp of self-loathing,

can become a repository of grief
   or desire we deny, or project,
      or helplessly attempt to erase.

Scotch and Sun

Home from night shift, my father
was too wired from fighting warehouse fires
to sleep— so he'd sip several Dewar's,
then rouse me for a morning at the beach.
There the combination of scotch and sun
would knock him out for a couple hours
while I invented tasks near the breakage—
skimming clam shells, counting one-legged gulls—
till he woke to hoist me onto his shoulders
and march into the sea, deeper with each step.
He'd look down to find a boy propped there,
his blazing, acceptable burden, his crown, almost
an abstraction shimmering from his skull,
some image of himself he once believed he'd been.
Then arch his neck to shut away the glare.
That noon I leaned too far back, back until my head
dipped into the combers, then below...
I struggled, thrashing my legs,
but my father clasped them tighter, closer
to his chest, oblivious, and went on
breasting the rollers, teasing the undertow.
Those broad shoulders eclipsed the sun.
Then hands grasped my hair— I was choking—
while my startled father stammered excuses
to the impromptu chorus of staring bathers.
He was more surprised than I, more scared.
He shook when he told my furious mother.
I simply had no idea, he said. Jesus,
that boy almost drowned
though I held him in my arms.

Betta Splendens

Black-bordered with electrician's tape,
the grief-heavy, navy, oversized drapes,
still sour with smoke from the funeral parlor
—a "gift" to my on-the-take father
whose hook-and-ladder had responded to the fire—
smothered all light, allowing him, home from night shift,
to sleep away the glaring winter noons.

By dusk the whole upper story was darker
than the sewers swallowing the broom-swept waters of Brooklyn,
each window muffled in sheaths of nuns' cloth,
nothing visible, the rooms torn from the planet
and swollen with the scorched air of the burn ward
where my father wept weeks later till his charred
hands healed into their scarred, starry shapes.

I lay in bed, afraid, straining my eyes to see,
past such absolute pitch, the flames that might envelop me.
No use. So I clenched my eyes tighter than fists,
screwing the lids shut like the lids of jars
until the pressure of pinched flesh
created bright bits floating in the vacuum,
needles of light evolving into miniature fish.

To hasten sleep, I'd begin to file
the names of each species swimming that ghostly mobile:
Siamese Fighter   Pearl Gourami
            Neon Tetra   Yellow Dwarf
Tiger Barb   Harlequin
till I'd awaken in some lesser darkness
and know, instinctively, another night had washed over me.

I guess I'd forgotten all this—
the depths of darkness, the caustic curtains, those imaginary
     fish—
when, last summer, swimming underwater
in hot springs near the Badlands, South Dakota,
I opened my eyes in the muted shallows
to a Morse code composed of light, pulsing
daubs in horizontal drift through the aerated froth.

That pool was filled with fish, brilliant and tropical,
the faded ochres of subterranean waters
blending with schools of sapphire, jade, and magenta.
Who hung these baubles there to swirl me
back to the soot-shadowed fabric of my family?
Some luckless woman, her second marriage failed,
tattered possessions tucked in the idling car...

that last evening she emptied the tank
fish by fish, scooping each dazzler with a net,
then spilling the rest into the spring, making
a small waterfall, a rainbow, in the hushed air.
And one fish, her favorite, the fighter, *Betta splendens*,
held itself at the basin's rim,
swaying its fanned tail, beautiful but stunned,

before bearing its single spark into creation.

III

Bountiful

Providence leads us to many tables
in our travels, to meetings with the insignificant
others who, placing olives on their tongues,
begin to shine like the swollen Buddha.

Watching them eat, we fill with desire.
The raw broccoli in its cradle of ice
quivers its antennae, breathing its green
and vinegary aroma into the room.

Lemons offer their soft, underwater light.
Pale crescents of peaches in Bordeaux,
cheeses defining the shaded meanings of *yellow*,
chunks of melon like the fabled jewels of pharaohs,

the breast of turkey whiter than the linen
wrapping the risen body of Jesus—
you know the kind of meal I mean.
When the bread is broken, love seems possible.

If the sleep that follows draws us away
from this life into another, more abstract landscape,
food eases us into a future
among friends, among the forbearing women.

And sorrow has no place at this table,
simmering in black pots on back burners,
or remaining in cookbooks
bought by husbands roaming malls after the divorce.

Snake Skin

Crumpled in a cold corner, soiled
silk stocking shredded along the seam
or rolled-up *Playbill* with shattered
spine, speckled scarf,
umbrella sleeve, cast-off condom— still
the skin startled me
before registering its papery vacancy.

Stencilled with faint brocade,
almost-white among wedding albums
and those few sparrows, stiff as brushes,
cloistered and bruised by battered windows,
the skin was charged with discovery
like a scroll in a sealed cave by the sea,
the parchment inked with pregnant ciphers.

Light-fingering it from the stashed
rubbish of the attic,
we looped it, tattered sash of crepe,
archetype's shadow, over the bedside table,
and listen now for nocturnal scrapings,
the mousing within the pantry walls,
the Darwinian preparations for winter

as she coils her lengths of boreal blood
tighter and tighter, knot of chafed leather,
glittering bracelet, palpable sin,
breathing through her newborn skin
the ceaseless constrictions of air,
ringing her corporeal chill
through the gauzy folds of the gathering year.

The Sadness of Barges

Often the barges revealed themselves 'round midnight
  with a groan like a tenor saxophone's,
    their slow scraping over the sandbars
  loosing gutteral, frog-tongued consonants
like our names throated beyond the bulrushes.

Then through the bedroom window we'd hear
  the watch's curses borne over the barnacles,
    and together bear the barges' great weight,
  their cargoes of coal and gravel and scrap
metal creaking as they caught in the current.

In those frost-lit hours longing overwhelmed us
  as we stared toward the vaporous green
    bulb announcing their narrow passage, a warning
  to ghost-rafts still drifting the previous century.
A man in love with literature couldn't help

But remember Gatsby's loss of the light
  signaling across the harbor, his heart
    a clock's counterweight rasping his ribs.
  Then the sadness of barges came clear
through the physical fog and fists of sweet basil,

Time suddenly palpable, each barge become
  the ponderous minutes taken to grind
    the bottom's hull-resistant stones, then
  the farther mound, the mossy moans grown longer
toward an impossible note held beyond breath—

Till my eyes left the light kindling the loud
  leaves to coax your eyes, to balance
    this ceaseless passage of barges,
  this history they haul from river to sound,
their burden the roar of this world we must bear.

Shhh

The language that remains unspoken, often
for years, till the shuddering rhythm of the Accord

helps to shape a stanza you revise aloud
in splendid isolation, becomes another version of *goodbye*

still less eloquent than Miles' muted "Shhh" on FM
& arriving much too late to make leaving easier for either.

"If I love you," wrote Goethe, "what business is it of yours?"
So the spondees that propel your dented shell this evening

begin to dissipate in the never-imagined future-without-her
like gasoline fumes floating from your fingers,

while those smoky solos— how she clasped you within her!—
resonate like the muffled clamor of orgasm, chords

blown beyond improvisation, beyond prosody, till
you surrender destination, your stress-laden vocabulary,

to the tires' susurration on the sodden leaves, & the slow,
unbroken seeping-upward of the combo. *Shhh.*

The Inarticulate

Touching your face, I am like a boy
who bags groceries, mindless on Saturday,
jumbling cans of wax beans and condensed milk

among frozen meats, the ribboned beef
and chops like maps of continental drift,
extremes of weather and hemisphere,

egg carton perched like a Napoleonic hat,
till he touches something awakened by water,
a soothing skin, eggplant or melon or cool snow pea,

and he pauses, turning it in his hand,
this announcement of color, *purple* or *green*,
the raucous rills of the aisles overflowing,

and by now the shopper is staring
when the check-out lady turns and says,
"Jimmy, is anything the matter?"

Touching your face, I am like that boy
brought back to his body, steeped
in the moment, fulfilled but unable to speak.

Lace

It was nothing, really, just a story
   overheard at some party, the speaker
     an attractive woman with a tattoo—
a miniature bluebird— bruising her left ankle.

How the hot needle had hurt, the bluebird
   swollen and suppurated, but—
     here's the part I can't forget—
how in the waiting room she'd thumbed

through glossy photographs of flesh
   the artist had illustrated,
     and come upon a torso
tattooed with a filigree of lace,

lace over breasts and back and waist,
   a blouse so fine-spun and subtle
     its bearer might slip among us,
not even the sober able to tell...

I don't know why this story
   stayed with me through cheap whiskey,
     the late hours, the heartbreak
of losing touch with a lover, but

I still can't shake the image of her
   below a lattice of wisteria,
     wearing nothing but light, milky
cursive, language sewn onto her skin

that I would begin to decipher,
   given the chance again,
     filament by filament,
until I might make sense of lace,

the ephemeral attachments that exist
   between one person and the next,
     between stories we embrace,
each story becoming our own.

Hummingbirds

When I read the translation from the Russian,
razdirat' dushu, literally, to "tear out" one's soul,
I understood the genesis of hummingbirds,
how they can be there and not-there,
how the specific wind of their wings
trembles the three leaves of the sassafras,
how the tumescent tongues of the lilies clamor their presence.

How the elements conspire to create them:
the blue-green pearl of molten sand
—that miniature globe, swirl of smoke—
hovering at the tip of the glassblower's rod
seems forever on the verge of cooling
into final form, the almost-shape of the hummingbird.

At the dinner party, no longer lovers,
we spoke to each other in such measured tones
to keep our voices from modulating,
until you couldn't help but choose
not to return my gaze, or respond to my mild jokes.
I felt some interior wall tumble away....

Who has ever seen a hummingbird arrive?

Who has seen a hummingbird at ease, though
its metaphysical dollop of flesh
must grow heavy, weighted with gravity, even
the saffron seed of its eye, the cork skeleton,
the heart like a ball bearing in its feathered case.

What I've never told you is that, beyond the ruins,
I glimpsed a garden
resplendent with hummingbirds,
an aviary of exiled souls
working so hard just to remain in one spot.

The Fox

After we peeled and dipped and sucked
each leaf of the artichoke
to reveal the fluted
heart still steaming in its shaggy
rind, after uncorking another light-proof
bottle of homemade plum wine, we began
telling our dreams, those that surprise us
or bring back the romantic
childhood urgencies long ago given over
to the conservative wishes of adults—
the wish to be simple, to hurt no one—
when, low to the earth, scavenging the frost-
lit bristles of sawgrass for torpid mice,
the fox appeared beyond the glass door,
tarnished silver, mottled with mange,
a rough rag torn from the hillside,
a storybook fox cut out with blunt scissors.
The retrievers shook off their sleep then,
ramming shoulders against the door,
slathering the thick panes with foam
till we hauled them, choke-chain, back.
The fox paused, gazing at the hushed
gathering only heartbeats away, then sidled off
into the muffled trees, leaving us
astounded, more than pleased, aware
of a mild blessing bestowed upon friends.
Later that night, I glimpsed our host's face
pressed to the guest-room window
while my wife and I undressed. Startled,
I yelled, and he quickly stalked away
between wavering stems of starlight.
During the awkward breakfast, he mentioned
how he'd gone out in search of the fox,
but found nothing but scat,
the autumn earth too hard for tracks.

Sometimes I dream of the fox in his lair,
that secret, interior life
growing thinner, losing hair, starving,
the alert intelligence sharpened by need
helpless not to transform itself into grief,
humiliation, the tense silence among friends
in return for a moment of mournful
revelation, the chimera of a child,
however naked and heart-rending, however
impotent and wild.

River Wife

During lovemaking he fell asleep, one moment
mindless, churning like a propeller,
the next fallen away like a corpse tossed over
the lip of a scow into a spoiled estuary.
But he floated on the surface, less flesh than oil,
and my mind was more alert now
than when we'd returned from the church social.
Cool light rinsed the room.
                            A sweet tongue—
the neighbor's who'd brushed past fox-trotters
to touch my arm, and I wished
I could have given myself to him wholly.
I was beginning to dream the trashy
novella, the intoxicating sin, the Ramada
on the bypass where the romance might begin,
the awkward undressing, then the minute
attentions to each yearning
ripeness of flesh
                        when the thumping began,
a distant sound that made me think
someone had entered the house and was stamping
booted feet. I almost woke
my husband by habit, but listened
to the dull reports— gunshots?—, then rose
to creep by ear to the summer porch,
then out into the yard toward the shed.
Frost stippled my skin
and the moon gazed frankly upon my nakedness.
The booming beckoned
though the shed door was bolted shut.
Rasping its hinge, I poked past shovels and rusted traps
to hear the thumping stop, then start.

A rubber barrel thundered each burst
and inching near I glimpsed the rat, larger
than a rat, nightmare of teeth and hair, berserk
with thirst and singular intent, leaping again and again
against the curved walls toward the impossible hatch.
I clamped the barrel with its lid, repulsion
rattling my ribs, secured the latch,
then hefted it to the barn,
the rat shifting but quiet now within.
I thrust the barrel into a stall.
But back in bed I couldn't sleep
as the furious thrashing resumed, someone
pounding a hammer across the river, someone
unable to stop the current threatening to sweep away her house.
I don't know when I fell asleep,
but by first light the noise had ceased.
I tramped to the barn through mist and slapping reeds
and removed the lid to find—
                              nothing.
The barrel was empty. The rat
had eaten through the rubber and slipped into the river.
That dawn I let what sun there was
strike me on the breast, absorbed the flame,
then turned to stare down the stagnant house
growing paler in the glimmer reflected off the river.

Village Dogs

1990

Groggy, we watched the ball descend
  as benediction upon the boisterous
    throng overflowing Times Square.
      We felt no desire

to mill there, to embrace the New
  Year among strangers, jostled and cold.
    Corks still popping at nearby
      parties, I leashed the dog only

minutes past midnight and let him lead me
  onto the village street, its one lamp
    a low moon lustrous below black
      clouds, glazed with rain.

What remained unspoken between us followed me
  like a shadow in a B movie, then sprang
    through a hedge-wall with a primal
      snarl. A pit bull, frothing

knot of muscle, slammed into my pet like a small
  train, tumbling him, his high-pitched
    yelps rising above their revved
      thrashings and the revelers' shouts.

I kicked and missed and thudded onto my back
  inches from their slathered, blood-
    slick snouts. *Match days of sorrow,*
      decrees Psalm 90, *with days of joy....*

I rose and dragged my broken dog
  by the choke-chain toward the house,
    the bull still clamped to his throat
      till I splintered a branch across its spine.

By now my wife stood pale on the porch
   as I hefted a brick to crush
      its skull, but her cry stopped my arm:
         "Don't. Haven't you done enough harm?"

The bull foamed in the hedge's shadow.
   I hurled the brick into its ribs
      and the creature— my stunted anger—
         fled with a groan. And when I returned

home, bruised and sober, the neighbors'
   festive clamor dwindling
      in the decade's first hour, who
         could deny that the marriage was over?

IV

The Torches

Nicaragua

Limbs lopped off, the fathers
thrashed through the orchard
till a torch was touched to their hair
and they were consumed by the unearthly
love that lifted their souls toward heaven.
How impossible to mute the body with belief.
Women closed their shutters and crossed themselves.
Soldiers jeered. But the burning were beyond
the grievous clamor of the New World.

Clear sky that night, the thousand stars
assuming tentative shapes
like children assembling in the schoolyard.
The ashes smoldered on the hillside.
Then rain. By morning, only chipped dice and the scorched soil
    remained.

What's irrefutable is that sweeping odor,
not the fume of charred tongues and gasoline,
but the first profuse blossoming of orchids,
a fragrant exhalation from the earth's core,
and those sudden shafts of light
crisscrossing in the late afternoon
as the missing bear through the marketplace
their flaming tapers of spine, their wicks of hair.

Paradys

"Of Paradys ne can not I speken propurly,
   ffor I was not there,"
      Sir John Mandeville joked in his *Travels*,

but in the six centuries of suffering
   since, the fortunate have been offered
      glimpses, rents in the archetypal

veil, fierce yet subtle glimmerings.
   I don't mean lovers, that sudden
      enlightenment as you're clasped

or kindled within, or museum-goers
   who envy Gauguin's Tahiti,
      or those minor poets who endlessly

exalt the vast stupor of childhood.
   No. I mean the multitudes
      who arrived by crutch

or bicycle or cart drawn by oxen
   or limb stunted since birth
      during the Festival of Lights—

who stooped to rest on the river
   frail boats of palm fronds,
      candles flaring silken cargoes

of lotus, then nudge them, gently,
   into the murmurous current
      till they caught and began

their spiraling descent, thousands of spirits
   conversant upon the waters
      in response to the beckoning stars.

Here, they seemed to answer,
  on earth where we belong....
    Then we drifted anonymously

back to the abandoned city,
  a procession of feverish
    visionaries, until we dispersed,

each to his solitary travels, to grief,
  despair, the sickness of the age,
    Mandeville mapping his route

beyond the 14th Century, the sinuous
  journey toward a once-glimpsed
    but by-now-extinguished Paradys

still issuing forth, a continuum
  of the faithful, each pilgrim participant
    if ever we desire to enter.

Chiang Mai
Thailand

The Book of Tea

in memoriam Kakuzo Okakura & for Jeffrey Skinner

Of the Bodhidharma, it is written:
"...when he found that fatigue caused his eyelids to drop,
interfering with his meditation,
he cut off his lids which turned into tea leaves."

I have several friends, nominal Zenists,
who practice less discipline with more feeling.
I can hear the ice-cubes clicking in their glasses
when they phone at night after the rates have gone down.

Such excesses are allowed in the search for enlightenment.

Of these several friends, there have been written
letters among their lovers, reviews of their slim volumes of
      verse,
and the occasional, brief obituaries that appear,
in black borders, on the inside covers of poetry journals.

And whom did the Bodhidharma disappoint—
father, lover, disciple?

*

"There is no single recipe for making the perfect tea.
Each preparation of the leaves has its individuality,
its special affinity with water and heat,
its hereditary memories to recall,
its own method of telling a story."

In the T'ang dynasty, the tea-cakes were dissolved
through the three stages of boiling:
"the first boil is when the little bubbles
like the eye of fishes swim on the surface;
the second boil is when the bubbles
are like crystal beads rolling in a fountain;
the third boil is when the billows surge wildly in the kettle."

Centuries later, the tea was reduced to powder, whisked
with split bamboo in the water of mountain springs.

Finally the tea appeared as we know it today, leaves
steeped in the white glaze of porcelain,
"froth of the liquid jade."

*

When I ignored the tea and got drunk at a party,
obnoxious in a charming sort of way,
the wiser woman told me:
"I'll sleep with you if you can remember my name."

I have saved that particular humiliation for the future,
hoping—
            through discipline and introspection, through
turning the eyes inward, away from their lids,
so that I might study the soul—
to learn at last to transcend my gender,
not to loathe the lonely woman who lives inside me,
and to see with the clarity of the Bodhidharma

who brewed a tea from the leaves of his eyelids,
let it cool, then inhaled it,
                                    one languorous sip,
while his meditation deepened:

on the simplicity of our earthly existence,
on the gentleness that sometimes surfaces in men,
on the pleasure of brewing tea in the spirit of forgiveness

which need outlast the lesser spirit of longing.

Leeches

In the northern provinces, the hill tribes—
  the Lahuna, the self-scarred Lisu—
    sold us bamboo shoots and sticky rice,
    puffs of opium drawn through bone-stemmed pipes,
and warned the guide to keep close watch
  during our village-to-village trek
    for tusked bush-rats, hooded cobra,
    and the long-clawed, foraging bear,
but only the smaller armies began to appear:
  leeches needling the eyelets of sneakers,
    the woolen weave of athletic socks.
Soon we found them in our hair, on eyelids,
rooting in the membrane under one woman's tongue
  as if they'd sprung from the constant rain,
    the mountain's mud, from nowhere.
These were not the thumb-thick, cinematic
leeches on Humphrey Bogart in *The African Queen*,
  but thread-like, less slick, persistent beyond measure.
  We burned them off with a mixture
of salt, limestone, and shredded tobacco,
then watched them writhe, alien and thirsty,
  while some among us could not stop
    grinding them into the earth,
  the leafy mold of the jungle,
hoping the leeches might disappear, hoping
  we wouldn't bear them back
    into the glare of civilization,
  those miserable crawlers, devil's whiskers,
charred splinters of bone, obsessive ideas,
  that in the future we might sleep
    with ears unplugged, mouths open,
  blood washing the brain's deep whorls
while we remain tethered to this world.

Chiang Mai
Thailand

Ticks

If I didn't take her ears
    between my fingers to stroke
        as women in department stores
    fondle Chinese silk scarves
to hear their lovely *hiss*, if
    I didn't riffle her mane
        to soothe her, whisper
    her name to hold her still,
I'd never locate the loathsome
    ticks, bloated beads
        of the witch's rosary,
    their almost-invisible heads
rooted in flesh. I twist them
    clockwise, counterclockwise,
        failing to remember the folk
    wisdom, then crack their shells
with a fingernail or drop them
    into the ashtray to burn.
        But by the time I return,
    seconds later, they're back,
such useless creatures, foreign
    feeders, God's bad idea, grappling
        hooks that never seem to let
    go, to disappear, blue obsessions
bulging below tufted swatches
    of hair, gorging there, growing
        fatter as the dog twitches
    in sleep, as I remove one
more, then another, then one more,
    women and silk fading now
        in the endless repetition
    of this task, the world gone
ugly, the voluptuous veneer rubbed
    raw, ticks inventing themselves
        now, imbedding their skulls
    below every smooth surface
to embrace us all, to bestow purpose.

Moray Eels

Dangerous tinsel, satin slash & slit, green
    ampules of dye spilling through sheer waters,
        the eels unsheathe their phallic flesh from coral
    to tear morsels of manta from the fists of divers
who risk danger for the pleasure of intimate encounter.

To coax them from their crannies,
    the dead skate is wing-grasped, then swished
        like a long-awaited letter from a distant lover
    till the eels, weak-willed, sleek forth
to clamp the flapping bait in traps of teeth.

Sometimes an eel makes a mistake, misjudges
    the wavery inches or, mean-streaked, doesn't,
        and bites the fist that feeds it— an old story,
    another painful lesson as the wound
soon festers with a rare, tropical fungus,

so the few tides after the news fans out
    no tourists tease them from their elkhorn chambers.
        Then, glitzy sleeves of habit, they swivel
    watery passages in search of generous strangers
till their splendor offsets their slender threat

and recent arrivals to the reef
    resume the tenuous tether to touch another
        creature who, beautiful, may turn on you
    as lovers sometimes do despite your chummy
motives, deep desires, or all-too-human gestures.

Ambergris Caye
Belize

Miles Weeping

To hear Miles weep
  for the first time, the notes bent
    back into his spent frame to keep
  them from soaring away—
I had to click the phonograph off
and hug myself to stop the shaking.
  I'd recognized a human cry
  beyond any longing given a name.
If ever he let go that grief
  he might not touch his horn again.
  That cry rose in another country,
  full-throated in awkward English.
I still have the envelope, unstamped,
  addressed to "Mother/Father," its oily
    scrap of paper torn from a primer,
  the characters like the inky
root-hairs scrawling the washed-out soil.
  Lek— every boy's nickname—
    wrote he was "to be up against,"
  meaning, I guess, that his future
was end-stopped, one unbroken line
of tabletops waiting to be wiped.
  He'd walked miles along the coast
  to find us combing the beach, then
stood, little Buddhist, with bowed head
  while we read his letter, composed
    with the help of the schoolmaster.
  How could we deny the yearning
ambition to abandon the impossible
  land of his fathers, to begin again?
  We could only refuse in a silent way.
  When someone asked Miles Davis
why he wouldn't play ballads anymore,
  he replied, "Because I love them too much."
  All that we never say to each other.
  The intimacies we can't complete.
Those ineluctable fragments. To be up against.

Koh Samui
Thailand

60

V

The Lost Civilization

Atlantis/Thira
for Robin

The lovers are sleeping on shorn sea-cliffs,
their balconies overlooking the black caldera
and those gaudy cruise-ships, toys in the harbor,
where lovers are sleeping in beds below water,

while below them the lovers-turned-stone are sleeping,
sifting through strata of alluvial beds, their
romance long-lasting, dead and living embracing
from the planet's amphora to the stars' milky hair—

while we wander the island at this odd hour,
the broken labyrinths and sandal-worn stairs
ghost-lit in the moon's diminishing aura,
kindling within us unspoken desire:

the missing, Minoan, night-flowing mirror,
the laval, erotic, God-showering fire.

Mosquito Nets

How they dawdle in the sea
breeze, water spouts
drawn to beds in stone cottages, furled now,
twisted and rising from the foam
mattresses, spellbound through nightfall.

Then, lamps extinguished, kerosene
fumes rending the honeysuckle,
the spumes open, dry leaves, dazzling webs
that sift the air, sway, then
begin to breathe, otherworldly.

Who would expect safekeeping
from tissue so sheer, so easily
torn by an outthrust arm or heirloom ring?
When sleepers succumb to the hazy
laws of lovemaking, the mosquitoes

pause in their trespassing
the precincts of lovers embraced all night
by the almost-invisible, lovers pleased
to mend, each morning, if they must,
their providential gauze.

Ios
1989

Scorpions

How easy, lazy in this light-struck country,
  to grow familiar with the morning
    rituals: boil water from the well,

hang the empty egg-basket on a nail
  for the frail farmer to fill,
    prop open shutters with rocks.

And rocks are more than abundant here
  where a man must shake his shoes
    like a nervous gambler at The Sands,

say, rattling his fist, then
  staring at what spills out—
    constellations of scorpions,

Rorschach blots come alive, the color
  of rancid butter, that yellow-going-to-brown,
    miniature skeletons awaiting flesh.

They click, broken dice, onto the stone
  floor, then scuttle into cracks
    before I bring the heel down.

Once I was stung on the thumb
  by a thimble-sized scorpion,
    and twice I've found two

locked together at the pincers,
  performing some arachnid mating
    magic or macabre toe-to-toe tango.

If you breathe on a scorpion,
  legend tells us, it burns bright blue,
    but whose lips would draw so close?

Yet who could consign even one
   to the lower concentrics of hell
      without regard to grand design?

Consider their power: to make a man
   meditate, ignore the sun
      to gaze into the shadows in his shoes.

Ios
1987

At Homer's Tomb

Ios

The precise spot where Icarus plunged,
    the harbor the ancient colossus straddled—
myth and history and geological quirks
    eased the task of political appointees
to the Hellenic National Tourist Bureau.
    Then they parceled out the ludicrous,
lesser-island landmarks by consensus,
    citing this barren upthrust of slag
as the burial ground of the revered bard,
    hoping tourists like squabbling gulls
might flock to the unconvincing plot.
    This low-level, congenial conniving took place
after the thousand wars with the Turks,
    the Nazi occupation, military junta,
that Greece might revive her dwindling drachma—
    not foreseeing nude beaches, gin fizzes, discos,
and clubs that loudspeaker classical crescendos
    by Dvorak, Schumann, Brahms and Vivaldi
as the sun wobbles down to drunken applause,
    nor the onset of that curious ennui
that afflicts jaundiced travelers ("world weary")
    who affix themselves to a garlicky taverna
to swap dubious sagas in resinous stupor.
    I sailed to this rock Sirens ago,
first by fluke, then beckoned back, despite
    money-fisted, barbarian hordes,
by bell-bearded goats on the mountainsides,
    by the wind-voiced, abiding spirit that dwells
near abandoned shepherds' huts and artesian wells,
    in the monolithic mantle of earth unchanged
despite land-rover rentals and sprawling hotels,
    and by this sojourner in the blood who yearns
for a marble-hard semblance of spiritual home.
    Like the hermit in a fairy-tale or poem,

I live in a stone cottage by the sea.
Do I grow strange in priapic proximity
to tawny, candescent, European lolitas
    who cartwheel and hand-stand in waist-deep
swells while tropes that prop the stranded soul
    with moral allegories of endurance
transform through Time and flesh to parody?
Last week two friends hove into sight,
having spanned an ocean for their summer visit
    to absorb the pure, Cycladic light.
On a walking tour of the island's churches,
    the husband, subject to unpredictable rages,
stomped off, alone, to their rented room
    in response to some gesture or misheard word
to fume immortalized, always-apt curses
    as if he might conjure a storm
while his wife and I scanned steep cliffs
    for chapels with Byzantine icons intact
and spoke of the love friends can't express
    when jealousy parches their spouses' spirits,
kindling a wick of unbearable grief
    in the soul-sick husband, the wounded wife.
By dinner he'd calmed, then apologized,
    and I loved him again like a brother
(here where shopkeepers mistook us for brothers),
    though they fled the island a few days later.
When their boat bassooned away from the harbor,
    both flailing and blowing kisses from the rail,
I wandered goat-paths across black hills
    in search of this neglected monument
to the blind, bountiful, Niotian poet
    who returned, near death, to his mother's home
to compose his unrhymed hexameters each dawn
    till interred with sorrow in this narrow

tomb marked today by a plastic water bottle,
   lemon rind and gulls' guano,
a local boy with shepherd's staff and horn
   —this story concocted by the Bureau—
for bored scholars on sabbatical to find.
When I die, let me lie in this stone
stunned by light, abandoned utterly, the Spartan
   beauty of the past breaking over me,
lost forever to family, lovers and friends!
Even Odysseus must have groaned with relief
when Helen was returned to her native state,
   leaving her homesick hero wondering
whether that woman ("Helen, thy beauty is to me
   Like those Nicean barks of yore,
That gently, o'er a perfumed sea,
   The weary, way-worn traveler bore") was worthy
to lend his life such unequivocal purpose, or
   was the reason for the Trojan War a bit overblown
like the romantic ideals we once placed faith in
   or tourist attraction that draws us from home
to fulfill a desire for meaningful diversion
   but remains nothing more than a gorgeous sham.